EMMANUEL JOSEPH

The Quantum Leap to Wholeness, Bridging Financial Independence with Personal Growth and Relational Wellness

Copyright © 2025 by Emmanuel Joseph

All rights reserved. No part of this publication may be reproduced, stored or transmitted in any form or by any means, electronic, mechanical, photocopying, recording, scanning, or otherwise without written permission from the publisher. It is illegal to copy this book, post it to a website, or distribute it by any other means without permission.

First edition

This book was professionally typeset on Reedsy.
Find out more at reedsy.com

Contents

1	Chapter 1: The Quantum Leap Begins	1
2	Chapter 2: The Foundation of Financial Independence	3
3	Chapter 3: The Power of Personal Growth	5
4	Chapter 4: Building Meaningful Relationships	7
5	Chapter 5: Bridging Financial Independence and Personal...	9
6	Chapter 6: Cultivating Relational Wellness	11
7	Chapter 7: Integrating Mindfulness into Daily Life	13
8	Chapter 8: The Intersection of Career and Passion	15
9	Chapter 9: The Role of Emotional Intelligence	17
10	Chapter 10: The Journey of Self-Discovery	19
11	Chapter 11: Navigating Life Transitions	21
12	Chapter 12: The Power of Positive Thinking	23
13	Chapter 13: Achieving Work-Life Balance	25
14	Chapter 14: The Importance of Physical Well-being	27
15	Chapter 15: The Path to Wholeness	29

1

Chapter 1: The Quantum Leap Begins

In a world of countless demands and expectations, finding the elusive balance between financial independence, personal growth, and relational wellness can feel like a Herculean task. Many of us embark on this journey without a clear roadmap, often stumbling upon moments of enlightenment or despair. However, with a holistic approach, it is possible to make a quantum leap towards wholeness, where financial freedom, personal development, and fulfilling relationships coexist harmoniously. This book aims to provide insights, strategies, and stories that will guide you on this transformative path.

Financial independence is not merely about accumulating wealth; it is about achieving a state of freedom where money serves as a tool for living a purposeful and fulfilling life. This journey requires a mindset shift, where one moves away from the scarcity mentality to embrace abundance. Personal growth, on the other hand, is about continuously evolving and expanding one's potential. It involves self-awareness, setting meaningful goals, and pursuing passions that bring joy and fulfillment. Relational wellness, the third pillar, is about nurturing healthy and meaningful connections with others, fostering a sense of belonging and support.

As we delve into this journey, it is important to understand that these three pillars are interconnected. Financial independence provides the resources and security to pursue personal growth, while personal growth enhances our ability to build and maintain healthy relationships. Similarly, fulfilling relationships offer emotional support and motivation, making the pursuit of financial independence and personal growth more rewarding and sustainable. By addressing these aspects collectively, we can create a life that is rich, fulfilling, and whole.

In the chapters that follow, we will explore practical strategies, real-life stories, and actionable steps to bridge these three dimensions. From financial planning and personal development techniques to building and nurturing relationships, each chapter will offer valuable insights to help you take that quantum leap towards wholeness. Whether you are just starting out on this journey or looking to enhance your current path, this book will serve as a companion, guiding you towards a life of balance and fulfillment.

2

Chapter 2: The Foundation of Financial Independence

Financial independence begins with a solid foundation, built on knowledge, discipline, and strategic planning. It is not an overnight achievement but a journey that requires consistent effort and smart decision-making. The first step towards financial independence is understanding your current financial situation. This involves assessing your income, expenses, debts, and assets to create a clear picture of your financial health.

Once you have a comprehensive understanding of your finances, the next step is to set clear and achievable financial goals. These goals should be specific, measurable, attainable, relevant, and time-bound (SMART). Whether it's saving for retirement, paying off debts, or building an emergency fund, having well-defined goals will provide direction and motivation. Additionally, creating a budget and sticking to it is crucial. A budget helps you manage your money effectively, ensuring that you are living within your means and allocating funds towards your goals.

Investing is another key component of financial independence. By investing wisely, you can grow your wealth and create multiple streams of income. It is important to educate yourself about different investment options, such as stocks, bonds, real estate, and mutual funds. Diversifying your investments can help mitigate risks and maximize returns. Consulting with a financial advisor can also provide valuable guidance and help you make informed decisions.

In addition to these practical steps, cultivating a positive money mindset is essential. This involves changing the way you think about money and overcoming limiting beliefs. Embrace the idea that financial independence is achievable and that you deserve to live a life of abundance. Surround yourself with positive influences, seek out financial education, and continuously strive to improve your financial literacy. By laying a strong foundation, you can set yourself on the path to financial independence and create a future of financial security and freedom.

3

Chapter 3: The Power of Personal Growth

Personal growth is a lifelong journey of self-discovery and self-improvement. It involves expanding your knowledge, skills, and abilities to reach your full potential. The first step towards personal growth is self-awareness. This means understanding your strengths, weaknesses, values, and beliefs. Self-awareness allows you to identify areas for improvement and set meaningful goals that align with your true self.

Once you have a clear understanding of yourself, the next step is to set personal growth goals. These goals should be challenging yet achievable, and they should focus on different aspects of your life, such as career, health, relationships, and hobbies. Creating a personal development plan can help you stay organized and track your progress. This plan should include specific actions, timelines, and milestones to keep you accountable and motivated.

Continuous learning is a crucial aspect of personal growth. This can be achieved through various means, such as reading books, attending workshops, taking online courses, and seeking mentorship. Surrounding yourself with like-minded individuals who inspire and challenge you can also accelerate your growth. Additionally, stepping out of your comfort zone and embracing new experiences can foster personal development and boost your confidence.

Another important aspect of personal growth is self-care. Taking care of your physical, mental, and emotional well-being is essential for sustained growth and fulfillment. This involves practicing healthy habits, such as regular exercise, balanced nutrition, sufficient sleep, and mindfulness. Setting aside time for relaxation and reflection can also help you recharge and maintain a positive mindset. By prioritizing personal growth, you can create a life that is aligned with your values and aspirations, leading to greater satisfaction and fulfillment.

4

Chapter 4: Building Meaningful Relationships

Meaningful relationships are the cornerstone of a fulfilling life. They provide emotional support, companionship, and a sense of belonging. Building and nurturing these relationships requires effort, communication, and understanding. The first step towards building meaningful relationships is self-awareness. Understanding your own needs, values, and boundaries allows you to connect with others on a deeper level.

Communication is key to any healthy relationship. This involves active listening, expressing your thoughts and feelings openly, and showing empathy towards others. Effective communication fosters trust and understanding, allowing you to resolve conflicts and strengthen your connections. It is also important to make time for the people you care about. Whether it's through regular check-ins, quality time together, or small acts of kindness, showing your appreciation and commitment can strengthen your relationships.

Setting healthy boundaries is another crucial aspect of relational wellness. Boundaries protect your well-being and ensure that your relationships are balanced and respectful. This means knowing your limits and communicating them clearly to others. Respecting the boundaries of others is equally important, as it fosters mutual respect and understanding. Building trust and reliability is also essential for meaningful relationships. This involves being dependable, keeping your promises, and being there for others in times of need.

Lastly, practicing gratitude and forgiveness can enhance your relationships. Expressing gratitude for the people in your life and acknowledging their positive qualities can strengthen your bond. Similarly, being able to forgive and let go of past grievances can pave the way for healing and growth. Building meaningful relationships is an ongoing process that requires effort and commitment. By prioritizing relational wellness, you can create a supportive and fulfilling network of connections.

5

Chapter 5: Bridging Financial Independence and Personal Growth

Financial independence and personal growth are two intertwined aspects of a fulfilling life. Achieving financial independence provides the resources and security to pursue personal growth, while personal growth enhances your ability to make informed financial decisions and create a life of abundance. Bridging these two dimensions involves aligning your financial goals with your personal values and aspirations.

The first step towards bridging financial independence and personal growth is to identify your core values and priorities. Understanding what truly matters to you allows you to set financial goals that are meaningful and aligned with your aspirations. This means not just focusing on accumulating wealth, but also considering how your financial decisions impact your overall well-being and personal growth. For example, investing in education or pursuing a passion project can contribute to both your financial security and personal development.

Creating a holistic financial plan is another important aspect of bridging these dimensions. This plan should consider your short-term and long-term goals, as well as your financial and personal growth strategies. It should include budgeting, saving, investing, and risk management, as well as personal development activities such as continuous learning, skill-building, and self-care. Regularly reviewing and adjusting your plan can help you stay on track and ensure that you are making progress towards your financial and personal growth goals.

Mindset plays a crucial role in bridging financial independence and personal growth. Cultivating a positive and growth-oriented mindset allows you to see opportunities for improvement and abundance in all areas of your life. This involves overcoming limiting beliefs, embracing challenges, and being open to new experiences. Surrounding yourself with positive influences and seeking out mentorship can also support your growth journey.

By bridging financial independence and personal growth, you can create a life that is rich, purposeful, and fulfilling. This holistic approach allows you to achieve financial security while continuously evolving and expanding your potential. It empowers you to live in alignment with your values and aspirations, leading to greater satisfaction and overall well-being.

6

Chapter 6: Cultivating Relational Wellness

Relational wellness is about building and maintaining healthy, meaningful connections with others. It involves fostering a sense of belonging, support, and mutual respect. Cultivating relational wellness requires intentional effort, communication, and understanding. The first step towards relational wellness is to prioritize your relationships and make time for the people who matter to you.

Effective communication is the foundation of relational wellness. This means actively listening to others, expressing your thoughts and feelings openly, and showing empathy and understanding. Effective communication fosters trust, reduces misunderstandings, and strengthens your connections. It is also important to be present and engaged in your interactions, giving your full attention to the people you are with.

Setting healthy boundaries is another crucial aspect of relational wellness. Boundaries protect your well-being and ensure that your relationships are balanced and respectful. This means knowing your limits, communicating them clearly to others, and respecting the boundaries of others. Boundaries create a sense of safety and trust, allowing you to build deeper connections.

Practicing gratitude and forgiveness can also enhance your relationships. Expressing gratitude for the people in your life can deepen your appreciation for their presence and contributions. Acknowledging their positive qualities and expressing your thanks can strengthen your bond and create a supportive environment. Additionally, practicing forgiveness can help you let go of past grievances and move forward in your relationships. Holding onto resentment can create barriers and hinder your ability to connect with others. By forgiving, you create space for healing and growth.

Building a support network is another important aspect of relational wellness. This involves surrounding yourself with people who uplift and support you. A strong support network provides emotional and practical support, helping you navigate challenges and celebrate successes. It is also important to be a supportive presence for others, offering your help and encouragement when needed. This reciprocity fosters a sense of community and strengthens your relationships.

7

Chapter 7: Integrating Mindfulness into Daily Life

Mindfulness is the practice of being fully present and engaged in the current moment. It involves paying attention to your thoughts, feelings, and sensations without judgment. Integrating mindfulness into your daily life can enhance your overall well-being and help you achieve wholeness. The first step towards mindfulness is to cultivate self-awareness. This means observing your thoughts and emotions and understanding how they impact your actions and interactions.

Practicing mindfulness can be achieved through various techniques, such as meditation, deep breathing exercises, and mindful walking. These practices help you stay grounded and focused, reducing stress and enhancing your ability to respond to situations with clarity and calmness. Mindfulness can also be integrated into daily activities, such as eating, working, and interacting with others. By being fully present in these moments, you can enhance your experiences and create deeper connections.

Another aspect of mindfulness is self-compassion. This involves being kind and understanding towards yourself, especially during difficult times. Self-compassion allows you to acknowledge your mistakes and shortcomings without self-criticism. It also involves recognizing that everyone experiences challenges and setbacks, and that you are not alone in your struggles. By practicing self-compassion, you can cultivate a positive mindset and foster personal growth.

Mindfulness also enhances your relationships by improving your ability to listen and empathize with others. By being fully present in your interactions, you can understand and respond to the needs and emotions of others more effectively. This creates a sense of connection and trust, strengthening your relationships. Integrating mindfulness into your daily life requires consistent practice and commitment, but the benefits are profound and can contribute to your overall well-being and wholeness.

8

Chapter 8: The Intersection of Career and Passion

Finding the intersection between your career and passion can lead to a fulfilling and purpose-driven life. Many people struggle to balance their professional responsibilities with their personal interests and passions. However, it is possible to create a career that aligns with your passions and values, allowing you to thrive both professionally and personally. The first step towards achieving this balance is to identify your passions and interests.

Understanding what truly excites and motivates you can provide clarity on the type of work that aligns with your values and aspirations. This involves exploring different activities, hobbies, and interests to discover what brings you joy and fulfillment. Once you have identified your passions, the next step is to find ways to incorporate them into your career. This may involve pursuing a career that directly aligns with your passions or finding ways to integrate your interests into your current job.

Networking and seeking mentorship can also support your journey towards a fulfilling career. Connecting with like-minded individuals and professionals in your field can provide valuable insights and opportunities. Mentors can offer guidance, support, and advice, helping you navigate your career path and achieve your goals. Additionally, continuous learning and skill development are essential for career growth and fulfillment. Investing in your professional development can open up new opportunities and help you stay competitive in your field.

Balancing your career and passion also involves setting boundaries and prioritizing self-care. It is important to manage your time and energy effectively to avoid burnout and maintain your well-being. This means setting realistic expectations, delegating tasks, and taking breaks when needed. By finding the intersection between your career and passion, you can create a life that is aligned with your values and aspirations, leading to greater satisfaction and fulfillment.

9

Chapter 9: The Role of Emotional Intelligence

Emotional intelligence (EI) is the ability to recognize, understand, and manage your own emotions and the emotions of others. It plays a crucial role in personal growth, relational wellness, and overall well-being. Developing emotional intelligence involves self-awareness, self-regulation, empathy, and social skills. The first step towards enhancing your EI is to cultivate self-awareness. This means understanding your emotions, triggers, and patterns of behavior.

Self-regulation involves managing your emotions and reactions in a healthy and constructive way. This means staying calm and composed during stressful situations, avoiding impulsive decisions, and practicing self-discipline. Developing self-regulation skills can help you navigate challenges more effectively and maintain positive relationships.

Empathy is the ability to understand and share the feelings of others. It involves listening actively, showing compassion, and being attuned to the emotions of others. Empathy fosters trust and connection, enhancing your relationships and creating a supportive environment. Practicing empathy can also improve your communication and conflict resolution skills, allowing you to build stronger and more meaningful connections.

Social skills are another important aspect of emotional intelligence. This involves building and maintaining healthy relationships, collaborating with others, and navigating social situations effectively. Developing strong social skills can enhance your personal and professional relationships, leading to greater success and fulfillment.

By developing emotional intelligence, you can enhance your personal growth, relational wellness, and overall well-being. It allows you to navigate life's challenges with resilience and grace, creating a more balanced and fulfilling life.

10

Chapter 10: The Journey of Self-Discovery

Self-discovery is a fundamental aspect of personal growth and overall well-being. It involves exploring your true self, understanding your values, and uncovering your passions and purpose. The journey of self-discovery is unique for each individual, and it requires curiosity, introspection, and an open mind.

The first step towards self-discovery is to create space for reflection and introspection. This means setting aside time to contemplate your thoughts, feelings, and experiences. Journaling is a powerful tool for self-reflection, allowing you to express your inner thoughts and gain clarity. Additionally, engaging in activities such as meditation, nature walks, and creative expression can facilitate deeper self-awareness.

Exploring your values is another important aspect of self-discovery. Your values are the guiding principles that shape your decisions and actions. Understanding your core values can help you align your life with what truly matters to you. This involves reflecting on moments of fulfillment and dissatisfaction, identifying patterns, and clarifying your priorities.

Uncovering your passions and purpose is a key part of self-discovery. Passion is the fuel that drives your enthusiasm and creativity, while purpose gives your life meaning and direction. Exploring different activities, hobbies, and interests can help you discover what brings you joy and fulfillment. Additionally, seeking experiences that challenge and inspire you can lead to new insights and opportunities.

The journey of self-discovery is ongoing, and it evolves as you grow and change. It requires patience, curiosity, and a willingness to embrace the unknown. By embarking on this journey, you can gain a deeper understanding of yourself and create a life that is aligned with your true essence.

11

Chapter 11: Navigating Life Transitions

Life is full of transitions, from career changes and relocations to personal milestones and unexpected challenges. Navigating these transitions with resilience and grace is essential for maintaining balance and well-being. The first step towards navigating life transitions is to embrace change as an opportunity for growth.

Change can be daunting, but it also offers the chance to explore new possibilities and reinvent yourself. By adopting a positive mindset and viewing transitions as opportunities for growth, you can approach them with confidence and resilience. This involves letting go of resistance and being open to new experiences.

Planning and preparation are also crucial for navigating life transitions. This means setting clear goals, creating actionable plans, and seeking support from others. Whether it's financial planning for a career change, organizing a move, or seeking guidance during a personal milestone, having a well-thought-out plan can reduce stress and increase your chances of success.

Building a support network is essential during times of transition. Surrounding yourself with positive influences and seeking support from friends, family, and mentors can provide emotional and practical assistance. Additionally, practicing self-care and maintaining a healthy routine can help you stay grounded and resilient.

Lastly, embracing flexibility and adaptability is key to navigating transitions.

Life is unpredictable, and being able to adjust your plans and expectations can help you navigate challenges more effectively. By staying open to new opportunities and being willing to adapt, you can navigate life transitions with resilience and grace.

12

Chapter 12: The Power of Positive Thinking

Positive thinking is a powerful tool that can transform your life and enhance your overall well-being. It involves cultivating a positive mindset and focusing on the opportunities and possibilities in every situation. The first step towards positive thinking is to become aware of your thoughts and beliefs.

Our thoughts shape our reality, and by becoming aware of negative or limiting beliefs, we can challenge and reframe them. This involves replacing negative self-talk with positive affirmations and focusing on the positive aspects of each situation. Practicing gratitude is also a powerful way to cultivate a positive mindset. By acknowledging and appreciating the good things in your life, you can shift your focus from what's lacking to what's abundant.

Surrounding yourself with positive influences is another important aspect of positive thinking. This means spending time with people who uplift and inspire you, seeking out positive content, and engaging in activities that bring you joy and fulfillment. Additionally, practicing self-care and maintaining a healthy lifestyle can enhance your overall well-being and support a positive mindset.

Positive thinking also involves setting meaningful goals and taking proactive steps towards achieving them. By focusing on your strengths and abilities, you can approach challenges with confidence and resilience. Visualizing your success and celebrating your achievements, no matter how small, can also boost your motivation and positivity.

By cultivating a positive mindset, you can transform your life and create a more fulfilling and abundant reality. Positive thinking is not about ignoring challenges but about approaching them with a solution-oriented mindset and a belief in your ability to overcome them.

13

Chapter 13: Achieving Work-Life Balance

Achieving work-life balance is essential for overall well-being and fulfillment. It involves finding a harmonious blend between your professional responsibilities and personal interests, ensuring that neither aspect of your life is neglected. The first step towards achieving work-life balance is to set clear boundaries.

Setting boundaries means defining your limits and communicating them to others. This involves establishing work hours, taking breaks, and prioritizing self-care. It also means learning to say no to additional responsibilities that may compromise your well-being. By setting clear boundaries, you can create a healthy separation between work and personal life.

Time management is another crucial aspect of work-life balance. This involves prioritizing your tasks, delegating responsibilities, and creating a schedule that allows for both work and personal activities. Using tools such as calendars, to-do lists, and time-blocking can help you manage your time effectively and ensure that you are dedicating time to both work and personal pursuits.

Practicing self-care is essential for maintaining work-life balance. This means prioritizing activities that nourish your physical, mental, and emotional well-being. Regular exercise, balanced nutrition, sufficient sleep, and mindfulness practices are important components of self-care. Additionally, setting aside time for relaxation and hobbies can help you recharge and maintain a positive mindset.

Creating a supportive environment is also important for achieving work-life balance. This involves seeking support from friends, family, and colleagues, and fostering a positive work culture. Building a support network can provide emotional and practical assistance, helping you navigate challenges and maintain balance.

By setting boundaries, managing your time effectively, practicing self-care, and creating a supportive environment, you can achieve work-life balance and create a fulfilling and harmonious life.

14

Chapter 14: The Importance of Physical Well-being

Physical well-being is a cornerstone of overall health and happiness. It affects every aspect of our lives, from our energy levels and mood to our ability to engage in daily activities and pursue our goals. Achieving and maintaining physical well-being involves a combination of healthy habits, regular exercise, proper nutrition, and sufficient rest.

Regular physical activity is essential for maintaining a healthy body and mind. It helps improve cardiovascular health, build and maintain muscle strength, enhance flexibility, and boost mental clarity. Finding an exercise routine that you enjoy and can stick to is key. This could be anything from running and swimming to yoga and dance. The important thing is to stay active and make physical activity a regular part of your routine.

Nutrition also plays a critical role in physical well-being. A balanced diet that includes a variety of nutrients helps support overall health and energy levels. This means consuming plenty of fruits and vegetables, whole grains, lean proteins, and healthy fats. Staying hydrated by drinking plenty of water is also important for maintaining physical health. It is also helpful to avoid or limit the consumption of processed foods, sugary drinks, and excessive amounts of caffeine and alcohol.

Rest and sleep are equally important for physical well-being. Quality sleep allows your body to repair and rejuvenate, supporting cognitive function, emotional health, and physical performance. Establishing a consistent sleep schedule, creating a relaxing bedtime routine, and creating a comfortable sleep environment can improve sleep quality. Additionally, taking breaks throughout the day and practicing relaxation techniques can help reduce stress and promote physical well-being.

By prioritizing physical well-being and incorporating healthy habits into your daily routine, you can enhance your overall quality of life. Physical health provides the foundation for pursuing your goals, enjoying meaningful relationships, and living a fulfilling life.

15

Chapter 15: The Path to Wholeness

The journey to wholeness is a continuous process of growth, discovery, and balance. It involves aligning your financial independence, personal growth, and relational wellness to create a fulfilling and harmonious life. By integrating these dimensions, you can achieve a state of wholeness where each aspect of your life supports and enhances the others.

The path to wholeness begins with self-awareness and intentionality. Understanding your values, priorities, and goals allows you to make informed decisions and take purposeful actions. This involves setting clear and achievable goals for your financial independence, personal growth, and relational wellness. Regularly reviewing and adjusting these goals can help you stay on track and ensure that you are making progress towards your aspirations.

Mindset plays a crucial role in achieving wholeness. Cultivating a positive and growth-oriented mindset allows you to approach challenges with resilience and optimism. This involves embracing change, overcoming limiting beliefs, and being open to new opportunities. Surrounding yourself with positive influences and seeking out continuous learning can also support your journey towards wholeness.

Balancing the different aspects of your life is essential for achieving wholeness. This means managing your time and energy effectively, setting boundaries, and prioritizing self-care. It also involves building and nurturing meaningful relationships that provide emotional support and connection. By creating a balanced and supportive environment, you can enhance your overall well-being and fulfillment.

The journey to wholeness is unique for each individual, and it evolves as you grow and change. It requires curiosity, commitment, and a willingness to embrace the unknown. By embarking on this journey with an open heart and mind, you can create a life that is rich, purposeful, and whole. The path to wholeness is not about perfection but about continuous growth and alignment with your true self.

The Quantum Leap to Wholeness: Bridging Financial Independence with Personal Growth and Relational Wellness is a comprehensive guide that explores the interconnectedness of three vital aspects of a fulfilling life: financial independence, personal growth, and relational wellness. This book offers practical strategies, real-life stories, and actionable steps to help you achieve a harmonious balance between these dimensions.

Embark on a transformative journey where financial freedom becomes a tool for living a purposeful life, personal growth leads to continuous self-improvement, and meaningful relationships provide emotional support and a sense of belonging. Each chapter delves into essential topics such as financial planning, self-awareness, mindfulness, and building healthy relationships, providing you with the knowledge and tools to create a life that is rich, fulfilling, and whole.

Whether you are just starting out on your journey or seeking to enhance your current path, this book will serve as your companion, guiding you towards a life of balance, fulfillment, and wholeness. Take the quantum leap and discover the potential within you to achieve financial security, personal growth, and relational wellness.

www.ingramcontent.com/pod-product-compliance
Lightning Source LLC
LaVergne TN
LVHW020503080526
838202LV00057B/6129